Treading Water

poems by

Constance Hanstedt

Finishing Line Press
Georgetown, Kentucky

Treading Water

Copyright © 2022 by Constance Hanstedt
ISBN 978-1-64662-766-0 First Edition
All rights reserved under International and Pan-American Copyright Conventions. No part of this book may be reproduced in any manner whatsoever without written permission from the publisher, except in the case of brief quotations embodied in critical articles and reviews.

ACKNOWLEDGMENTS

Grateful acknowledgment is made to the following publications in which these poems or earlier versions first appeared (sometimes with different titles):

California Writers Club Tri-Valley Branch Anthology, *Voices of the Valley:* "The Altar;" "Dear Dad;" "Moving On;" "Bay Beach"
Calyx: "The Ice Fisherman"
Las Positas College Anthology, *Beyond the Window:* "After 35 Years;" "Beginnings;" "Taking Inventory"
Naugatuck River Review: "The Bath"
Poppyseed Kolaché: "Luau Night;" "Seventh Street Park"
Porter Gulch Review: "Proof;" "The Note"
Red Wheelbarrow: "Lilacs"
2018 California Writers Club *Literary Review*: "Waiting for the Fishermen;" "Night Watch"
The Comstock Review: "Acceptance"
University of Wisconsin—Fox Valley, *Fox Cry Review:* "The Bridge Tender"

Publisher: Leah Huete de Maines
Editor: Christen Kincaid
Cover Art: Photo by JK, unsplash.com
Author Photo: Monique Rardin Richardson, photographer
Cover Design: Elizabeth Maines McCleavy

Order online: www.finishinglinepress.com
also available on amazon.com

Author inquiries and mail orders:
Finishing Line Press
PO Box 1626
Georgetown, Kentucky 40324
USA

Table of Contents

Acceptance 1

Proof 2

Bay Beach 3

The Altar 4

The Note 5

Make Believe 6

Beginnings 7

The Ice Fisherman 8

The Bridge Tender 9

Waiting for the Fishermen 10

Just Married 11

The Bath 12

Layers 13

After 35 Years 14

Moving On 15

This House 16

Lessons 17

Dear Dad 18

Taking Inventory 19

Luau Night 20

One More Time 21

Night Watch 22

Dear Mom 23

Seventh Street Park 24

Lilacs 25

*For my children,
Ryan and Cara*

Acceptance

I'm two driveways from home
and wonder when the ash overtook
the yard, shade soaking the grass
like dark honey.

Its trunk has raised the earth
and the circles of dandelions at its base,
bright yellow heads of hope.

I remember how my father mowed
his weeds flat, yanked roots
with his right hand
efficient as a pickax.

I never felt the urgency
to demand only goodness
from the living.
I never took a leather strap
to the bare skin of my son,
or slapped my daughter across
her wide-opened mouth.

This is your sanctuary,
I say to the land.
Leave your mark,
a ragged trace,
a path of imperfection.

Proof

How innocent we look,
three children in the faded photograph.
On the left a boy of five with blond
crew cut and straight-ahead stare,
lips unbending and resigned.
On the right a girl two years older
whose light brown curls bounced
until the warning to *Just sit still a minute.*
So she calmed herself, her curls settling
around the wide curves of her mouth.
On their laps a baby is propped,
her eyes fixed on a distant point,
her open mouth round and silent.
We were freshly scrubbed, spotless
like just-cut gardenias.
The boy started fights with neighbor kids,
pummeled the arms of his little sister,
and felt the slap of his parents' anger.
The girl drew hopscotch squares
on the narrow sidewalk, then dashed
beyond the backyard boundary
of thick raspberry bushes.
And the youngest child surveyed
her world as if a wary visitor, unsure
of her importance while treading
timidly through rooms of butter yellow.

Bay Beach

His broad chest was cocoa-colored,
as were his feet, spread wide
like glimmering monarch wings.

With overall cuffs rolled to match his,
I stood tall to meet his sagging pockets.
In front of us, perched in tufts of grass

dotting the cool moist sand, an empty
beer bottle sparkled the same glorious
amber as the stained-glass image

of St. John during noontime Mass.
A string dangled from my fingers
to the bottle, *A fishing line*, he said,

and I held it tight with lofty expectations.
My uncle laughed loud and long,
the creases in his face glistened.

I giggled as our bodies tumbled to
the ground, a heap of dampened limbs.
I marveled at his huge white teeth,

brilliant like flickering rows of votives.

The Altar

To honor our holy Mother on the first
of May, my brother smoothed foil
on his bookcase and transformed it
into an altar, a meager replica of the one
at St. John's where elderly nuns placed
pink carnations.

Mary graced its center, her youthful skin
draped in folds of blue as tapers glowed
and gilded angels prayed like children
at the Communion rail.

My brother and sister knelt before them.
Bow-tie stiff he clicked rosary beads
between earnest fingers. And she smiled
ever-so-slightly, head bowed over prayer
book and ivory dress of dotted Swiss.

I squeezed between them, stunned
by the unaccustomed silence.
Did they ask for Mary's guidance?
Claim innocence when I knew better?
Neither paid attention to me, not while
my toes burned in black patent leathers,
not when my arms ached from his rapid
punching. I stared at Mary's naked feet.
I'll go to Confession every Saturday.
I'll recite one hundred Our Fathers.
If only I could sustain the silence.
If only I could be tough like them.

The Note

My darling, Connie, her note began.
The thought that followed, before the final
Love, Mother, simply stated she'd be home
in a few days. I knew better. Her bed
was neatly made, yellow sheets tucked tight,
embroidered quilt smooth over foam pillows.
Navy pumps stood in her closet beneath
a perfect row of belted knits. No, she'd be gone
for a while. There was, after all, the matter
of her handwriting. I imagined her propped
at our table the night before, fingering the lump
in her throat, clasping a dull number two
and forming letters only slightly resembling
her usual crisp cursive. The lower case 'o'
endured the weight of capital 'C' before
collapsing onto the double 'n's, and 'ie'
melted into a tiny puddle. I wondered if
she wrote her goodbye so I couldn't watch
the lump moving up and down with each
raspy syllable like a fisherman's bobber
on the Fox River. Neither of us had to fuss
over the other: no last minute warnings of
Pick up your toys and *Listen to your father*,
no wiping of wet cheeks as the Buick spun away.
I set her note on the edge of my nightstand.
My darling consoled me for five June days.

Make Believe

In Pam's garage on summer mornings,
I primped Barbie's platinum bob, yanked
a black-and-white swimsuit over her
plastic breasts, and wondered how it felt
to be a woman. I imagined loud parties
with boys, *Be My Baby* playing on the hifi,
and punch bowls brimming with sweetness.
Maybe I'd kiss a Ken in the corner and then
brag later to friends. Or sit by the door
when shyness froze my bones. *Speak up!*
Mom used to say whenever I stared at my feet.
So I practiced on Barbie, although she lived
in a Dream House without a bitter mother
or silent father who drank too much
and set the world on fire. *Put your feet up
on the coffee table*, I said to Barbie.
Sip this pink lemonade and breathe.

Beginnings

Speed it up, my sister yelled
over her shoulder, ponytail bouncing.

At fourteen she thought she was Natalie Wood
in black stretch pants and fur-trimmed coat,

too old to walk me to the library.
Do I have to? she asked every Saturday.

My pink Keds smacked the concrete
behind her toward Main,

the air carrying wood smoke
and rust-colored leaves, my arms swinging

with abandon. When she pulled open
the heavy library door, sighing with her effort,

I strode passed her and the card catalog,
gleaming under fluorescent globes.

I lingered among glossy pages of birds
and mammals from Africa,

took comfort in the librarian's perfume
and the ink of her stamp pad.

When my sister said, *Hurry, just pick one,*
I jammed a stack into the crook of my elbow.

On the way home my braids brushed
the Maytag sign on the glass of Druck's Electric,

and I reveled in the first glorious crack
at freedom.

The Ice Fisherman

In January the fisherman hammered
loose nails on his wooden shanty, then
dragged it onto Lake Butte de Morts,
a glacier-carved, frozen finger of the Fox.
Bundled in wool muffler and fur-lined
parka he began his day's work,
and sometimes, I was his helper.
With blond braids wound tightly under
knitted mounds of bright green yarn,
I shared the foggy breath of the patient
ice dweller. He scraped and drilled,
lines were dropped, and thermoses
of brewed coffee and steamy cocoa
warmed our tired gloved hands.
Snuggled under red plaid blankets,
we sat on orange crates in the dim
shanty for hours, waiting to snag
a slithery creature from beneath
our rubber-soled feet. His husky voice
praised the talents of our baseball heroes,
Hank Aaron and Warren Spahn,
and I longed for a County Stadium,
mustard-soaked hot dog and the glare
off the third base dugout.

The Bridge Tender

On rainy days he stayed inside
the square stone bridge house
and listened to a Cubs game

or scoured the sports page
for current league standings.
I envied his answer-to-no-one

time: when the world kept
moving, and he, sipping coffee
hot and black, did not.

Instead his flannel shoulders
leaned lazily against the threshold
while the Fox River below,

like his archaic lawn mower,
churned and spat a thick green
mist at the rock-lined shore.

When the rain subsided,
he studied the parade of cabin
cruisers as he expertly lifted

and dropped the drawbridge.
He waved heartily, shouting
What a fine day, then fixed

his gaze on the age-old river
as it consumed the last
of the shimmering specks.

Waiting for the Fishermen

The just-before-supper sun flickers
through a dusty basement window
as I sit alone on cool concrete
between cases of soda pop
and Pabst Blue Ribbon.
While the old washer thumps,
stubby bottles of grape
and my coveted cherry march
gingerly in cardboard squares.
Their taller counterparts rattle
violently, until I fear explosions
onto Mom's laundry, hanging
stiff-sleeved and bleached
above me.

Only a pine table breaks ranks,
shoved from a corner to the center
and news-papered for fish gutting.
I imagine the raucous scene—
my uncle chopping one-eyed heads,
Dad slicing bloated bellies.
This time, I'll escape the slaughter,
race up the steps where Mom
quietly flours pink slabs and lays
them in a buttered skillet.
At the table I'll pretend we've said
grace, ask Dad to pick out the bones,
place a piece of perch on my tongue
like Holy Communion.

Just Married

At twenty, when girls my age
still slow danced at the Raveno,
I learned how to live with a man.

In a third floor walk-up close to campus,
I arranged my cheap shampoos alongside
his English Leather and divided
our tiny closet into two equal spaces.
Rent devoured all of our money.
A paltry price for heaven.

Most nights, as the radiator sputtered,
we studied on our gold velvet sofa
under Browning's "half-moon large and low."
Later, despite *Black Magic Woman*
blasting from across the hall, we sank
into each other like slender threads of rain
on the window ledge.

But on Friday nights, a dollar bought
two beers and ping pong at the student
union, or Cokes at Billy Mitchell Field.
Lying in the back of our Pinto wagon,
we closed our eyes and dreamed of
takeoffs into the blazing Midwest sky.

The Bath

She saw my naked body
that languid September morning
just a few short hours
after my son's first breath.

Why can't they help you?
my mother asked, waving
her freckled arm at a herd
of pony-tailed nurses whose
sturdy white shoes marched
in and out of rooms where
soft-voiced women nestled
pink newborn limbs.

I'm not the only one, I laughed,
handing her my soiled gown
as I lowered muscle-pulled
calves, thighs, sagging belly
into the steaming sitz bath.

Through the humid air drifted
rumblings of *Nurses in my day,*
while milk-warm water soothed
my skin, a rosy reflection of hers.

She saw my naked body,
spread wide a graying towel,
and shared the latest gossip
of her weekly poker club.

Layers

At first our lips can't get enough.
They search until their soft centers fold into
each other like cream whipped, blended,
and veiled in angel food layers.
Then they open, and I feel everything. Teeth.
Crevices. The bumpy ridge grazing my tongue.
It's all I can do to steady myself. Like a small
girl twirling in her mother's frayed blue skirt
with willow legs that glisten in the humid night air.
Nothing pulls her away. Not the mosquito's buzz.
Not the mother's jolting, *How much longer.*

But these days, our lips rarely touch.
They are burdened with slammed doors
and *Oh my Gods,* numb with all the moments
we can't talk about. Even if I want to, I can't
put my feet back on solid ground. Like a child
struggling beyond the sea's edge, her muscles
cramp. She screams while thrashing leaden
arms. Holds her breath when water tastes
like black earth.

And isn't this how it always goes?
A sudden blush, the yanking in, the dance
of a thousand lavish moons? Until we expect
too much. Accept blame for faults we never
knew we had. Dream of starting over again,
then again, fresh and strong as newborns.
Welcome lips as if there were no others.

After 35 Years

He makes me feel old and used up,
like the neighbor's dog, relegated
to the outdoors and redwood deck
twenty feet beyond my window.

With winter fur matted and gray,
you'd never know Aki is one of those
large white breeds except for his ears,
cocked and luminescent in midday sun.

As boys whiz by on scooters,
he pokes his snout through gaps
in the gate and moans, a low sorrowful
plea for freedom.

I want to stroke his sturdy chest,
coo *Good boy* over and over until
he quiets, until strength steels his bones,
those quivering legs beneath him.

I'll let him run through new grass,
sniff rosemary and moss, chase
crows from the gutter. I'll skip behind
and lay claim to the earth, cheer
the wild plum pulse in our veins.

Moving On

I wrap our Candlewick dishes in newspaper
and remember last Thanksgiving,
pumpkin pie passed from hand to hand,
the clicking of forks on plates, and you,
sulking in the hallway like a small boy
punished for bad manners.

I place the box by the others, recall
our third floor walk-up near campus,
your chest nuzzled against my spine
as cheap gold curtains billowed
from gusts off Lake Michigan.
Thirty-five years later and I still hear
the scuttle of cockroaches and
your voice, *We'll get a better place soon.*

The phone rings. I know it isn't you,
just as I know the hawk perched
on the light pole will swoop
over the redwoods that you claim
spoil the view. It's easy to part
with some things:
a watercolor from Venice,
wine glasses from Napa,
teak dressers and king-size bed.
Now sun pounds our double pane
windows, anoints the sixty-inch TV
I won't take.

This House

In the dining room, a three-foot pine stands
atop the wine cooler. A snow village consumes
the baker's rack, glittered greeting cards line
the wet bar, and stacked presents await opening.
When I lived alone, I did my best, propping a fake
six-footer in front of the window after my son said
Macy's is having a sale. Instead of hundreds
of white icicles hanging from the eaves, I sprinkled
two strings of colored lights along the bushes
and marveled at my home. With a mortgage
and utility bills. A battered fence that I was sure
would topple over in the next storm. Sometimes,
triumphs are simple. A tray of sugar cookies.
A tin of fudge. My voice, singing *Silver Bells*,
with all its cracks and imperfections.

Lessons

I'm pinching tomato plants and basil,
pruning the purple morning glory
as hummingbirds dip and dive on currents
of memory. I smell the damp earth
and recall my father's muddied hands
digging in his garden. *Never crowd seeds
together,* he said. *Give them room to grow.*
It was his confidence I loved then,
his hearty laugh, his cotton rolled-up sleeves
swiping sweat from his brows. Now,
as I fill a watering can, I see him sprinkling
his neat rows while eyeing the raspberries
that separated our yard from the next.
All summer I picked crimson clusters
before supper, when humid air retreated
and my skin felt the first cool rush of evening.
Sparrows settled in the maple, and the earth
grew quiet. As my father lounged in our
screened-in porch with his pipe and a book
on his lap, I understood the importance
of a job well done. Shoulders lightened.
Breaths deepened. Muscles softened like
silky threads of moonlight. Fifty years later
and I still remember his voice, coaxing
tomatoes and carrots to rise, praising
soft rains, their tender ballads of hope.

Dear Dad

I remember when we hiked High Cliff
above churning Lake Winnebago.
You didn't speak as fall wind swept
the ridge and hickories shook their
heavy limbs, spewing a red as radiant
as the Sacred Heart beating on my
classroom wall.

You scoured the cool damp earth
for hickory nuts, your flannel sleeves
erasing dirt from hulls like white gloves
swiping grimy faces at noon Mass.
You chuckled at your good fortune,
whistled as gray squirrels scurried into
the underbrush. My hands held so few
yet you said, *Whatever you can find.
That will be enough.*

I know now your silence had nothing
to do with me. It was your way,
how you navigated a world of three
children, monthly bills, rotating shifts
at the paper mill. Dad, it was enough.
Your broad smile, your clear blue eyes
gleaming like the sunlit waves below us.

Taking Inventory

I have to toughen up, my sister stammers,
as we fall onto the front seat of her Ford wagon,

her ruddy complexion flushed by August heat.
You're tough enough, I say stunned

by her self-reproach and my hasty response,
for surely I could offer kinder words.

After three days of cataloging Mom's
belongings, I am consumed by memories:

the dusty picnic table around which we sang
to Dad as he blew out his last birthday candles;

the kitchen pantry emptied of stale crackers
and soups, the staples of her existence;

the dark brown sofa I choose to sleep on,
disregarding her empty bed as an option;

the assisted living center where she wakes
and screams at the roommate looming

over her bed. *We're doing our best,*
I finally say to my sister, hiding my grief

deep inside, like Dad's navy pin buried
beneath Mom's tarnished bracelets.

Luau Night

Palm tree banners greet the party goers
who sit in long neat rows with polyester legs

turned politely to the evening's entertainment.

A few clap their blue-veined hands
to the pulsing drums while others

offer a simple toe-tapping.

Shiny strands of plastic petals grace their
sweatered chests, lustrous reds and yellows

ablaze like strips of downtown neon.

Mom doesn't sit with the others. She stands
off to the side, staring at the front door

as though waiting for someone.

Her eyes narrow and lips purse
as if she's just detected the lack of salt

in her ham and split pea soup.

One More Time

I didn't order this! my aunt wails,
wrinkling her unruly gray brows
as the waitress slides a personal pan pizza
before her. *Yes, you did,* I say matter-of-factly,
nodding at the steaming cheese and sausage.
It's a repeat of last night at the Third Street Diner,
when cream of broccoli soup with its tiny green
specks was declared foreign and indigestible.
I picture my wheel-chaired mother
in the Alzheimer's unit with eyes sealed shut
like ancient tombs, jaw locked and blouse
yellowed by futile attempts to feed her.
Is this what I'll become, mourned
by my children even though I'm still breathing?
I declined my doctor's offer to be tested.
One drop of blood, I told him, wouldn't get me
to Paris any sooner or speed up plans to remodel
the house I'd recently moved into. Now my aunt
swipes tomato sauce from her chin. I tidy up
the table, pay the bill, and step outside,
basking in the odd comfort of excessive heat
and humidity. Will times like these keep me
from going crazy? Will they be enough?

Night Watch

I hunch near my mother's bed
in the curtained vestibule
as I have all day,
straining to hear her breath,
or catch an eyelid flickering
in the yellowish gauze of light.

It's hard to believe she is dying:
no tubes, no trickle of fluids,
no monitors, not a blip of promise,
nothing.

She lies straight as a ruler,
doll-like, gray and weightless.
Even her mouth is still,
lips dry as ancient bricks.
Absurd, this archive of memories
caulked.

I want her to open her eyes, bark
Sit up straight, you'll ruin your back.
She used to stand behind me and yank
my shoulders, two strong knobs
that knew no tenderness.
I want to be a girl again,
lose myself in her white silky hair,
the fleshy dark pit of her neck.

Dear Mom

Judy still has your music box, although
its tiny brass feet now rest on a dark-stained
table instead of the third shelf of a crowded
oak bookcase, its home after you died.
I imagine you prefer this spot just inches
from a foot-wide photo of Dad, chin up
and shoulders back handsome in a white
Navy uniform and cap angled on his forehead,
smooth as honey.

Remember your bedroom on State Street?
Summer mornings I laid on your butter yellow
sheets, eyeing the music box as you scurried
through your daily routine. I slowly raised
its red-jeweled lid, afraid I'd break it, afraid
of your temper, hot and quick like grease
in a cast iron skillet. Then, miraculous relief
as chiming and an uncommon tenderness
warmed my skin. *Don't wind it too tight,*
you said, zipping your steel gray knit.
Just once more, as you slipped on silver bangles.
After you left for work, I wound the box over
and over, falling asleep with it safely tucked
in the crook of my elbow.

I wonder now if Judy could part with it.
But I don't ask. I lie on my bed as heat rises
each morning and imagine my fingers
caressing the music box, its melody soothing
every muscle, every weary bone.

Seventh Street Park

In this black-and-white on the mantle,
he pushes her on a swing. Fresh from Sunday service
or their daughter's noon meal. She's a trim seventy
yet everything about her is large: peonies burst
on her belted dress, pearl clip-ons, iridescent bulbs
on her ears, straw hat trellised by dried blossoms
and vines as if to say we still live.
She's one-handing it, neck and pumps
stretched to the wind, grinning widely, the creases
on her face like furrows of soft sand.
Behind her he's got a death grip on the metal.
Plain white shirt cuff-linked at his wrists,
black eyes peer through wire frames,
burning the camera's lens.

Oh, how opposites attract.
Oh, how some just learn to let go.

Lilacs
    for Rob

Here, at eye level, are the last of the lilacs.
Not a heady purple, but a quiet color,
a lavender as muted as Grandma's soap
after weeks of washing. And they're not
the luscious bunches she'd display
in tall green jars on her windowsill!
These lilacs are the remnants of spring,
holding on despite restless branches,
surging stems, roots with lungs of foremen
in steel-toed boots barking, *Let's keep
the line going.* On this May evening
I draw them near, capture their will
to keep on living, their brief shadow
of perfume.

Constance Hanstedt was born in the Midwest and earned a bachelor's degree in English and Secondary Education from the University of Wisconsin—Milwaukee. She worked as a substitute teacher and proofreader before moving to California. For thirty years she was co-owner and CFO of a general contracting business in Pleasanton.

It wasn't until after her father died in 1993 that Constance discovered the healing power of poetry. Since then her poems have appeared in numerous literary journals and anthologies, including *Calyx, The Comstock Review, Naugatuck River Review, Rattle, Porter Gulch Review, Red Wheelbarrow,* and the California Writers Club *Literary Review*. Her poem, "An Ode to Beige," was published in *The Crafty Poet, A Portable Workshop* by Diane Lockward in 2013. Hanstedt's first book, *Don't Leave Yet, How My Mother's Alzheimer's Opened My Heart* (She Writes Press, 2015), was named a finalist in the memoir category at the Pacific Northwest Writers Conference in 2011, and a finalist in the National Indie Excellence Awards in 2015.

Constance lives in Livermore, California. She is a member of the California Writers Club Tri-Valley Branch, leading the Poetry Critique Group and serving on the Executive Board. To learn more about Constance, visit www.constancehanstedt.com.

www.ingramcontent.com/pod-product-compliance
Lightning Source LLC
LaVergne TN
LVHW041518070426
835507LV00012B/1651